TAMING THE
ELEPHANT
MIND

Lama Choedak Rinpoche

*A handbook on the theory
and practice of Calm
Abiding Meditation*

Published in Australia in 2013 by
Gorum Publications
PO Box 3430 Manuka ,
Canberra, ACT 2603 Australia

Website: www.sakya.com.au
Email: mail@sakya.com.au

First published in 1996 as "Notes on the Theory and Practice of Shamatha Meditation". Fully revised and renamed as "Taming the Elephant Mind - A handbook on the theory and practice of Calm Abiding Meditation" in 2013.

Second edition September 2013

Reprinted with new cover and formatting in August 2016

ISBN: 978 0 9945813 0 3

"A life of only a single day
spent in meditation
conjoined with wisdom
is better than living a hundred years
unbalanced and confused."

The Tibetan Dhammapada

TABLE OF CONTENTS

Preface--i

Calmness is in our Nature--1

The Origin of Calm Abiding Meditation----------------------------3

The Four Foundations of Mindfulness --------------------------------5

Doing - Knowing - Seeing - Feeling --------------------------------8

Preparing for Meditation-- 11

Mindfulness of Body – Seven Point Vairochana Posture ------- 14

Meditation and Motivation-- 21

Reflections on Calm Abiding Meditation ------------------------ 24

Mindfulness of Feeling - Watching the Breath------------------ 27

Pain in Meditation -- 31

Meditation on Pain-- 33

Obstacles and their Antidotes - Part I--------------------------- 35

Mindfulness of Speech--- 41

Meditation on Blessing One's Speech --------------------------- 43

Everyday Mindfulness -- 45

Walking and Standing--- 48

Obstacles and their Antidotes - Part II ------------------------------- 50

Five Experiences of Calm Abiding Meditation ---------------------- 55

Nine Mental Stages of Calm Abiding Meditation-------------------- 59

Balancing Compassion and Wisdom---------------------------------- 67

Prayers for the Practice of Calm Abiding Meditation --------------- 69

Shakyamuni Buddha Mantra --71

Developing the Motivation to Meditate ----------------------------- 72

Meditation on Death and Impermanence---------------------------- 78

About the Author --83

Meditation Centres --- 86

PREFACE

Mindfulness and meditation are two aspects of the Eight Fold Noble Path taught by the Buddha in 500 BC. Buddhists have been practising these for many centuries and have made a valid contribution to create peace in people's lives. Today people think Buddhist teachings are scientific, logical, practical and sensible. Buddhism does not need science to prove the authenticity of its teachings. It only needs people to engage in meditation and promote it as such, without watering it down for the purposes of mere stress reduction and performance enhancement. A large number of people have taken on what is known as *Mindfulness Based Stress Reduction Therapy* and it has been promoted as if it was developed by someone in recent years, without giving credit to the teachings of the Buddha. Elsewhere, others try to promote the same by calling it *Compassion Based Stress Reduction Therapy*. The form of meditation the Buddha taught and practiced is called 'Calm Abiding Meditation' and it is the remedy for all 84,000 afflictions - not just stress. The teaching of the Buddha is *wisdom based* reduction and elimination of all afflictions and sufferings.

This handbook consists of notes compiled primarily to accompany the *8-Week Course on Calm Abiding Meditation* that I conduct for students of Buddhism and the general public. I have been conducting these courses for over 18 years. There are also many of my students who have been facilitating this course on a regular basis throughout Australia and New Zealand. Nowadays, a few Tibetan Buddhist centres are starting to offer classes on Calm Abiding Meditation, but they are usually taught as a philosophical explanation of the topic without devoting any time to sit in quietness and do the practice of meditation.

i

Over the years I have adapted these courses to provide practical techniques for the general public. It is not necessary to hold any religious beliefs in order to benefit from Meditation. Calm Abiding Meditation might also be useful for people of other faiths who wish to enrich their religious life.

You will gain the most benefit by practising every day, even for just a few minutes, rather than from longer occasional bursts of enthusiasm. Even when you are not meditating formally, you can carry the benefits into your daily life by doing everything with a sense of purpose and a gentle attitude. Enlightened experiences do not necessarily occur only on the meditation cushion. You may have such an experience walking to the shops, provided you walk along with a calm, clear and stable mind!

Calm Abiding Meditation tunes our minds to the wave length of spaciousness, freedom and happiness. If you desire these qualities, may you find them by following the practices contained in this booklet!

Lama Choedak Rinpoche

Calmness is in our Nature

Unruly beings are as unlimited as space
They cannot possibly all be overcome.
But if I overcome thoughts of anger alone
This will be equivalent to vanquishing all enemies.

Where would I possibly find enough leather With
which to cover the surface of the earth? But
wearing leather just on the soles of my shoes
Is equivalent to covering the earth with it.

Likewise, it is impossible for me
To restrain the external course of things.
But should I restrain this mind of mine
What would be the need to restrain all else?

Shantideva

We learn more about life by actual experience than through many years of theoretical study. Meditation is an ancient spiritual technique which enables people to discover true happiness for themselves. Happiness is not to be found in external things. Although we do feel pleasure when we obtain longed-for objects of desire, that pleasure is short-lived. Like children bored with our new toys, we soon tire of material things. Indeed, we may later spend as much energy in ridding ourselves of them as we once spent in acquiring them!

Practicing meditation leads us to the fundamental realisation that all things are transitory.

Calm Abiding Meditation or *Shamatha* suits people of all walks of life. We all want calmness and stability, qualities which will serve as our best friends throughout life. This technique emphasises the importance of being gentle towards ourselves. If we are gentle with ourselves we will also be gentle with others. Once we learn to achieve calmness, we can transform our environment into a peaceful place. We rediscover our sense of harmony. We cultivate the inner wisdom eye, which enables us to see the beauty all around. With our new calmness and wisdom, we become empowered to solve our own problems. We can transform ourselves and our perceptions, rather than expecting others to change or to solve our problems.

We all have an instinct to be calm and to create calm. There is never a time when we do not wish to be calm. Calmness is in our nature; it is in the hearts and minds of every one of us. However, calmness should not be confused with inaction. It is not a fearful, timid or passive thing but rather it is active, innovative and transformational. We can only cultivate calmness through understanding the causes of agitation and by deliberately choosing to transform such agitation into a calmer state of mind. A person who is not calm does not have time to choose right from wrong or safety from danger. Calm abiding is the safest way of being. It is, in fact, active peace.

To learn Calm Abiding Meditation techniques we must understand that most of the time we are calm, but we have to learn to abide in that state without becoming distracted. Observing that the mind is calm and not being distracted by any external stimuli will allow us to dwell in a state of calmness.

Calm Abiding Meditation techniques help our minds to become relaxed, focused and peaceful. This enables us to recognise the causes of our unhappiness and to recover from stress, anxiety and tension. Learning to have Calm Abiding as a way of being helps us to remove undesirable habits, improves our confidence and adds a touch of dignity and sacredness to our life.

THE ORIGIN OF
CALM ABIDING MEDITATION

The stream from the snow peaked mountain is pure.

Tibetan Proverb

Meditation was practised in ancient times by Indian sages known as *rishis*, who spent many years in solitude. They sacrificed material comforts and exercised great devotion and discipline. Many people misunderstand such practices as a path denying enjoyment. It is impossible to achieve the ultimate benefits of meditation without withdrawing the attention to some degree from material things. When Prince Siddhartha left his palace in Kapilavastu, he headed for a place of solitude, away from all distraction. After learning the basics of meditation, he reduced his intake of food, withdrew from other activities and went to sit still in meditation. The form of meditation practice he engaged in was sitting calmly and observing the chosen object of meditation to achieve one pointed concentration. In this way the Buddha himself spent six years practising Calm Abiding Meditation, culminating in his enlightenment under the Bodhi Tree.

Those who steadfastly practise meditation observe the changing nature of all phenomena and learn to lose attachment and aversion to sensory objects. They discover that the objects of anger and attachment are merely a creation of their own mind - this is the reason why their minds previously lacked calm and inner peace. Through meditation, one knows that all sensory objects, both animate or inanimate, are transient and illusory and that it is easier for the consciousness to rest in calm and tranquility. The aspiration to attain enlightenment for the benefit of all, yields far greater passion than the energy one previously directed towards sensory objects. In meditation, it becomes so obvious that all the miseries one experiences are created by the mind under the sway of afflictions. Recognising this important fact by paying attention through Calm Abiding Meditation, the meditator learns to moderate his afflictions and withdraw his projections.

Calm Abiding Meditation is the most fundamental of all forms of Buddhist meditation practice. It has long been respected as a secular method for developing peace and calm. The human mind has a huge capacity to see things more clearly only if it learns to pay undivided attention. By practicing Calm Abiding Meditation, one simply learns to calm the minds incoherent thoughts and emotions by focussing one's attention with simple and practical techniques. The attention is focused to co-ordinate with consciously doing, knowing, seeing and feeling. One starts with sitting to find a way to experience stillness - observing without distraction. If one does something calmly, while consciously knowing and seeing what one is doing, then one feels at ease observing peace in stillness.

Calm Abiding Meditation is a technique to tame the mind so that one knows how to be gentle with one's thoughts, feelings and emotions before expressing them. In doing this, one will be able to pause thoughts and emotions consciously, without facing the danger of being swayed by them and feeling a need to react.

Nowadays, Buddhist mindfulness techniques are being employed in psychology, alternative therapy and the health industry to assist people to cope with difficulties in a sane and calm manner. It is a very safe practice for people of all walks of life. It is the way to find inner peace and understanding.

just mere thoughts. This is the process translated as Mindfulness of Thought.

Mindfulness of Thought will be enhanced by learning to become accustomed to practicing Qualified Rounds of Breath. When one is mindful of one's own thoughts, it is easy to see why they are empty on the other side. If the mind is not observed in the mind, then the question, "do any of the thoughts exists at all?" arises. The thought is there to be known, but it lacks any independent existence. It is clearly seen but empty in reality.

Mindfulness of Phenomena

When one is at the level where one can see the clarity of the mind and thoughts, all phenomena are understood to be merely designated concepts, labelled by our mind. It is our perceptions that determine the way our sight, smell and taste etc. engage with their respective sense objects. This is able to be rebooted. Objects do not have inherent existence but are totally empty from their side - the other side of our perceptions. The art on the canvas may appear on one side, but on the opposite side it is empty of the art. Even the art is a mere designation of the mind.

All phenomena can be observed simply, like space. In the clear mirror of the meditative mind, one can see all the empty reflections. They appear like a rainbow or an illusion and to hold them to be real is what causes all the problems. They are not only unreal but are transient and do not last long. At this most subtle level, one cannot be mindful of the emptiness of phenomena without Calm Abiding Meditation.

Doing - Knowing - Seeing - Feeling

*Meditation is so confronting because it brings us
to the very causes of suffering.*

Lama Choedak Rinpoche

Meditation is often mistaken for a vacuous, thought free mental state. The body can be temporarily made comfortable and dulled through relaxation of the senses. Relaxation has its place and might be regarded as a byproduct of Buddhist meditation, but dullness is not a cause of happiness in the long run, let alone liberation and enlightenment. In Calm Abiding Meditation, we address the suffering caused by afflictions and ignorance by applying the attributes of doing, knowing, seeing and feeling to our meditation. The interpenetration of these four attributes enhances the quality of Calm Abiding Meditation without any of the obstacles.

Doing

It is said that Buddha did what had to be done for the benefit of all sentient beings. Practicing meditation may require getting out of bed a little earlier or sitting in an unfamiliar posture, perhaps with a sore bottom at times. Real satisfaction comes from doing something that is well conceived and settled on at the beginning and followed through to it's fruition. As the word sitting has a very passive connotation, we may replace it with *sit-doing*, active and present in the act of sitting. If it is walking, then it should be walking to walk, instead of being distracted by where one wants to go.

Knowing

It takes time to know what we are doing. Reading, writing and arithmetic are second nature, but there was a time when we had to train in the form and rituals until we knew, beyond any doubt, the *how* and the *why*. Knowing brings into the path a conscious process of familiarisation. With time we can get used to anything. Knowing what we are doing and for what purpose empowers us and we can inject renewed energy and effort in our practice.

Seeing

Buddha's meditation was very insightful. He perceived ignorance as the root of all suffering. He was able to see the inner working and effects of his meditation. In meditation one checks and scrutinises the quality of our attention in order to avoid the faults of dullness or agitation. When one checks what one is doing, one becomes more aware and understands the obstacles which in turn becomes useful friends. If one is so present in the act of conscious doing, then one can witness how seeing becomes believing.

Feeling

Compassion for others who do not understand their suffering and how it arises goes beyond sympathy. The ultimate benefit of practice and retreat is the feeling of liberation from our deluded perceptions. We become fit to give and share joyfully at all times.

Mindfulness requires us to check whether or not the thing we are doing is being done wilfully and in the best way. There is no shock in revealing mistakes, because the keen person will not idealise doing without mistakes. Doing, knowing, seeing and feeling are meditative attributes we can apply to every activity that we undertake, including our work, washing the dishes or cooking.

Preparing for Meditation

A journey of a hundred mile begins with one step.

Japanese Proverb

Having the right conditions for meditation is important if we want to maximise our ability to meditate effectively. Just as we need the right conditions to undertake most of the activities in our lives, to practise meditation we also need certain requirements or conditions. Traditionally, six prerequisites have to be observed to successfully practice Calm Abiding Meditation. They are: (1) finding a conducive and agreeable place, (2) having few desires, (3) having few activities, (4) knowing how to have contentment, (5) good self-discipline and (6) discarding discursive thoughts. In reality, these are more like the results of Calm Abiding Meditation.

In any case, it is important to have some of the following basic supporting factors to do Calm Abiding Meditation:

Find a peaceful and conducive place to meditate

If we live on our own, this will not be difficult. If we live with others, and especially if we live with our family, some negotiation may be needed to set aside a place where we can sit without intrusion or interruption. More accomplished meditators might find a `retreat' in the midst of nature, far from the numerous distractions of daily life, in which to meditate. The importance of an environment and a place that is conducive to practice meditation should not be ignored. This is why the Buddha left home and sought a peaceful place to do his meditation.

Arrange a space reflecting our desire to cultivate calmness

The space we create might include some flowers, a lighted candle or an image of spiritual significance. We might care to burn incense or fragrant oils to help us establish a calming ambience. If we are devoted spiritual practitioners, we might choose to practise meditation in the presence of a simple shrine, with inspiring spiritual images or symbols to help instil a positive state of mind. We also need a meditation mat, cushion or seat, which may be a stool or an armless chair for those who find it difficult to sit in a cross-legged position.

Allocate a specific time to meditate

This is one of the most important requirements for a meditation practice. In the beginning, we may only spend 15 to 20 minutes sitting in meditation. This will gradually increase as we become familiar with the practice and the benefits it brings. The regularity of our practice is even more important. If we can commit to meditating daily, we will gain a significantly greater benefit than if we meditate only sporadically. It is also important to assign a time of day to meditate. Many practitioners find meditating in the early morning is a more effective time for their practice because their minds are not so stimulated with the distracting thoughts of the day.

Establish a positive motivation for your meditation

Simply reflecting on the benefits of cultivating calmness and mindfulness, such as reduced stress levels, greater tolerance of difficulties and improved relationships with others, can help us to establish a state of mind conducive to our meditation practice. However, the best motivation we can cultivate is the desire to be of assistance to others, and that through our meditation practice, we will enhance our ability to help bring them happiness and free them from suffering.

Reinforce your motivation reciting inspiring words or verses

For those with a spiritual inclination, reciting prayers or spiritually inspired verses will be beneficial. Reading the *Reflections on Calm Abiding Meditation* in this book as a preparation for meditation will help us to arouse an appropriate motivation for our practice. According to Kamalashila, one should take refuge in the Triple Gem and recite the Seven-fold Prayer before engaging in the actual meditation.

MINDFULNESS OF BODY – SEVEN POINT VAIROCHANA POSTURE

Learn to sit in the correct posture.

Lama Choedak Rinpoche

There are seven main characteristics of the meditation posture. They are named after Buddha Vairochana, who embodies the form of all the Buddhas.

1. Legs are crossed in diamond Posture

Sit on a soft and comfortable seat with your legs in the lotus, or diamond, posture. This nurtures the quality of *stability*.

This posture shapes your bottom and legs into a triangle, which symbolises the *Womb of Enlightenment*. It also represents the *earth element*. Once you become accustomed to this posture, it will give you a feeling of groundedness, as if you were in direct contact with Mother Earth. You will get to know her qualities of endurance and stability. Mother Earth is the source and support of all that exists in the world. When the Buddha sat under the bodhi tree on a mattress of simple kusha grass, pledging not to move from that posture, the earth shook six times under the force of his resolve.

Physically, it is said that our effusive energy can be controlled by the cross-legged posture. Interlocking the legs expresses harmony between all dualities, including you and the rest of the world, as well as between the mind and body. It is the wedding ring that represents the marriage between your spiritual self and the physical body.

Spiritually, this body posture expresses one's confidence and determination. This is how we used to sit when we were babies. It was only later in our lives that we learned to sit on chairs, sofas and more recently lazy chairs and bean bags.

Consciously *doing* the cross legged posture, *knowing* that it represents the firm earth of confidence, *checking* that the posture is guarded, and *feeling* grounded in the task at hand is the main meditation.

2. Hands equally placed in the meditative gesture

Place your hands on your lap, with the back of the right hand flat on the left open palm, and the inside of the tips of the thumbs upraised and gently touching each other, about two inches below the navel. This posture induces a feeling of *equanimity*.

By resting your active right hand, representing masculinity, on top of the passive left hand, representing femininity, you begin to cultivate balance and harmony. This is analogous to a carefully coordinated flexing of two wings in preparation for travelling into the space-like freedom of enlightenment. It expresses a withdrawal from extremes of emotion and symbolises the search for spiritual contemplation.

On the spiritual level, this position of the hands signifies an aspiration to transcend dualism. It symbolises the indispensability of uniting compassion and wisdom, not striving for one without the other.

Pressing your thumbs together below the navel, which is the centre of psychic heat, you control your thermal energy. The ten most important subtle veins of our bodies are located at the tips of our fingers. Bringing these veins together in the lap is essential for developing meditation.

This hand gesture represents the cohesive and absorbing qualities of the *water element*. The meditator will moisten his mind by keeping this gesture so that any signs of rigidity and slackness are washed and the thirst of equanimity is quenched.

The importance of the hands is illustrated when we shake hands with another person. We intuitively learn something about the other person simply through the hand contact.

Consciously *keeping* the hand gesture, *knowing* that it represents the cohesion of balance, *checking* that the gesture is guarded and *feeling* harmonious in maintaining the task is the main meditation.

3. Back is straight like an arrow

Keeping the backbone straight, with the vertebrae upright to extend the entire body, while having a deep sense of increasing awareness, induces the mind to be wakeful and attentive and nurtures the quality of *clarity*.

The central channel is very subtle and is located within the physical spinal column. Maintaining a straight, upright back allows both the subtle airs and the blood to flow easily. If the body is kept straight, the veins will remain straight. When the veins are straight, the subtle element known as bodhicitta nectar will flow unimpeded and the mind current will also flow freely. The main message here is the importance of keeping the back straight throughout meditation.

A straight back represents awareness and radiance coming from the flame of the *fire element*. The nature of a flame is ascending, radiating upward and giving light. The fire of effort consumes the fuel of laziness.

Remember that posture controls the diffusive energy of the body. Correct posture symbolises our spiritual clarity, confidence and a resolute attitude towards our practice. Think of the importance of shooting a straight arrow if we wish to hit the target!

Consciously *keeping* the back straight, *knowing* that it represents the radiance of fire, *checking* that the back is straight and *feeling* bright and sharp in maintaining that, is the main meditation.

4. Elbows and shoulders are like the wings of an eagle

Straighten your elbows and shoulders evenly. This position synchronises and harmonises all the elements of the body posture.

Model yourself on a eagle flexing his wings before taking off. This sustains the vital energies by promoting full expansion of the lungs during meditation.

5. Neck bent and chin slightly tucked in

Press your chin downwards slightly to allow the neck to bend slightly forwards. This posture coordinates the position of the head to the rest of the body, particularly the shoulders.

Do not bend your neck to either side, or backwards. This would produce unwanted heat in the upper part of the body which could cause sluggishness and drowsiness. A slight forward bending of the neck, on the other hand, helps to channel the ascending energy and guards against coughing, sneezing and burping during meditation.

6. Tongue touches the palate

The tip of the tongue should touch the upper palate, with the teeth barely meeting and lips kept natural.

This position helps to avoid extreme dryness and wetness occurring within the mouth and allows the cooling breath to pass freely between the teeth. Meditators who forget to maintain this position may fall asleep during the meditation or may dribble. There are more advanced mouth postures which so effectively promote the blessings of physical vitality that one does not need to eat any gross food.

Actually, our bodies are by and large made weary by our continuous consumption, processing and discharge of gross food. Just imagine that by keeping your mouth in the correct posture you will not only reduce feelings of hunger, but save on your grocery bill at the same time! When you experience hunger, you can simply let your tongue imbibe more fresh saliva from the upper palate, which will keep you going for quite a while. Do not neglect the tongue posture - it is very important to the success of your meditation.

7. Eyes focus on the tip of the nose

The eyes should gaze serenely into the space a little beyond the tip of the nose, without the eyes moving or blinking. This aspect of the posture is nurturing insight.

You are not focussing on anything in particular, yet at the same time you are not avoiding anything, either. Never shut your eyes while meditating. To do so is considered very inauspicious in the Tibetan system of meditation. My teacher always opened his eyes as widely as possible during visualisation meditation. If you shut your eyes, it may induce sleep and even spoil your mouth posture.

The eyes are very important. You can tell a lot about another person by looking into his or her eyes. This gaze represents the *air element* bringing fresh oxygen to the brain. It brings lightness and spaciousness to the head. Keeping the eyes in the correct gaze also helps to relax the facial muscles, and will remove wrinkles caused by worry and anxiety.

Our eyes contain the nerves which govern discursive thoughts. It is therefore crucial to control them by maintaining the correct gaze which will help to control all the secondary energies, revitalise the nervous system and reduce blood pressure, stress and anxiety. It also helps to evoke spiritual energies and stabilise your regenerative fluids, particularly the seminal fluids in their respective planes.

Consciously *keeping* the correct gaze, *knowing* that it represents the view of insight, *checking* that the gaze is guarded and *feeling* light and introspection in maintaining the task is the main meditation.

Summing up the importance of physical posture

There is deep mythical symbolism in the *Sit*. Even sitting outside of formal meditation sessions can induce calmness. When people are trying to resolve something carefully and quietly they will sit. Those who pace up and down and throw their arms about are not interested in a compassionate outcome from a middle way approach.

A steady meditator will spend three quarters of the meditation session just correcting the physical posture. When you maintain correct posture, you will achieve physical and mental harmony which will safeguard you against illnesses. Your complexion will appear radiant and your skin will be soft to the touch. You will avoid the need for plastic surgery and for the reliance on the cosmetic world of materialism. Amongst the eight precepts Buddhists adopt on certain special occasions or retreats, one is to refrain from using cosmetics or wearing jewellery. It is not that Buddhists do not want to look attractive. It is rather that they wish to cultivate the beauty of the inner self, which will eventually shine though. To quote an old Tibetan proverb "If the flower has fragrance, it will attract the distant butterfly."

Instead of meditating on the traditional thirty-two disgusting aspects of the physical body to remedy desire, it is more productive and meritorious to learn to scan and meditate on the the Seven

Point Vairochana posture. While there is merit in meditating on the foulness of the body, it is important to have the inspiration to sit up as a disciple of the Enlightened One and at least pay tribute to his enlightenment, which he achieved through sitting in this very posture.

Meditation and Motivation

May all beings have happiness and the cause of happiness
May they be free from suffering and the cause of suffering
May they never part from the happiness that knows no
suffering
May they dwell in equanimity free from attachment and
aversion to those near and far.

Four Immeasurables - Buddha

Meditation leads to a clearer mind, better motivation, improved conscience and more competence in what we do. It is important that we ensure we don't bring harm to others in the process of meeting our own needs. Often we don't know what causes we are creating so we don't get the results we expect when they mature. What meditation does is to give us the clarity to examine the motivation of our actions.

We need to be able to examine our thoughts and motivation before things are executed. If not, it is too late and we may be compelled by pre-existing habitual patterns. Meditation reconditions our motivation. When our meditation is improving, then we will examine our motivation beforehand (the causal motivation) and our motivation at the time of actualisation (the action motivation). These two motivations are often not the same and that can be a cause of conflict.

It is important to have the ability to withdraw - restraining from doing what is not beneficial to others. We need to be more aware of what we are doing - always. The mind can be a careful inspector, rejecting negative impulses such as jealousy, hatred and so on. These negativities can be physical, verbal or mental. If we reject negative impulses and become calmer, we don't lose to distractions.

Prayers are designed to help us tune our motivation. "May all living beings have happiness and the cause of happiness" and so on. Clarity will also improve our motivation for meditation Meditation is therefore a constructive way of praying and helping people and it arouses the heart, but it has to come from the heart to make a difference.

If our motivation is narrow we are much more likely to be disappointed by whether or not we have a straight back or whether there must be no noise in the room when we meditate, and so on. It is important to widen our horizons in order that our mind gains an insight into a reality that is more than normally apparent. This removes the veil - we are no longer hindered from seeing the truth. Previously, self-oriented reasons have been causes of suffering but if our motivation is correct we don't just meditate to bolster our idea of "self". When we try to tune our minds to have an altruistic motivation before we act, then everything widens to develop sincerity and kindness.

Good motivation leads to respect, kindness and love, and then small acts can even be a cause of happiness. Someone who is able to be calm, peaceful and without haste can do simple things and be an example to others. One whose meditation is developing will be looking for the small things that help others.

Our way of being in meditation carries over to the rest of our life, but it requires concerted effort to constantly do this. Try to relate better to those around you. This means operating with good will and carefulness. Try to be mindful of others. Consider the carer and the cared for. There is no certainty that happiness comes from what one does, unless it is done with good motivation.

Meditation minimises our desires. We eventually become able to correct our motivation and have greater clarity and awareness in what we do. If we do things with an exalted motivation to benefit others this will take us above our own selfish purposes. We will have a more effective meditation and our endurance and tolerance will increase.

REFLECTIONS ON CALM
ABIDING MEDITATION

Recite before each meditation session -

My mind has long been lost in search of happiness,
Without knowing how transient all things are.
Seeing the unsatisfactoriness of real life experiences,
I will not let my mind wander outside.

Turning back the forces of harmful habitual inclinations,
And holding firm to the peace and tranquility within,
I rejoice in the store of joy I have discovered
in the happiness of observing the intrinsic calmness.

Let this clear and luminous nature of the mind
Not be overshadowed by my habitual tendencies,
Abiding in the natural calmness of the mind
Let me see all perceptions as nothing but mere reflections.

Neither grasping nor rejecting any sensory perceptions,
I shall see them as adventitious ripples and waves
Of the sea of my mind in deep meditation
And absorb them into the ocean of clear mind.

As I focus my mind to sit in the correct meditation posture
Let the physical self express the deep yearning
To experience the calm, still and spacious nature of the mind
And transcend the problems I have with this body.

The incoming breath brings in all the positive things outside me
And permeates the whole nervous system of my body,
Like the rays of the morning sun dispelling the darkness
It soothes the pain and temporary discomfort.

As I retain the breath, let me sustain
The vital energy of wakefulness and alertness,
Enabling me to let go and forgive the past
And to enjoy the fresh manifestation of this bare moment.

My outgoing breath releases all feelings
Of tension, anger, stress, anxiety and worry.
Like the masses of dark clouds suddenly disappearing,
Let the adventitious circumstances elapse to dawn a new beginning.

Breathing and observing the bare moment of awareness
Without assuming what it will become,
May I live every moment with pristine awareness,
Without waiting for an unforeseen future to cultivate it.

Following the wise sages by respecting their words of wisdom,
Let me remember skilful ways to apply them in everything
I do, say and think, so that my conduct brings no harm to others
And I do not become a victim of what I do, say and think.

While watching the constant flow of thoughts
Without discriminating between those that are good or bad,
Let me neither be overjoyed with my meditation
Nor depressed by my lack of concentration.

Sinking in a withdrawal of the senses
Is relaxation of the conscious self, but not meditation.
Let me not be excited by the slight virtues of concentration
I have just begun to experience.

Holding the rope of mindfulness and the hook of alertness,
May I resolve to tame this mind, which is like a wild elephant.
Steadily focusing the mind with a moderate application of antidotes,
May I discover what causes its restlessness.

When I find no sensory objects which are not my own reflection,
All visions and experiences are circumferences of myself.
Like trees, mountains, rivers and the earth
My existence is to give and share what I have with others.

How can I cling to and grasp what I have obtained from others?
As soon as I let something go, I create space and experience joy.
As soon as I give things away, I find a joy not found in keeping them.
Learning to cherish others will bring me a happiness that will last.

Mindfulness of Feeling - Watching the Breath

Having first stabilised our bodily posture, as discussed previously, we can now turn our attention to the breath.

Instruction

To begin, we simply note the cycle of our breathing. First we feel the breath entering our body, the *inhalation*. We may feel the sensation of breath as it enters the body at the tip of our nose, or we may note a sensation of movement of the breath at the top of our throat or in the movement of our diaphragm.

Next we become aware of the *abiding* phase of the breath, the pause or space between our inhalation and our exhalation. We may initially find this phase of the breath difficult to distinguish from the end of the in-breath and the beginning of the out-breath, but as our meditation progresses and we relax into our breath ,the pause between our inhalation and our exhalation will lengthen.

The third part of the cycle of our breath, the *exhalation*, follows when our body recognises the need to expel waste air. Again we may feel the movement of air outward from our body in the diaphragm, the top of the throat or at the tip of the nose.

Qualified Rounds of Breathing

To begin with, focus for a few minutes on simply becoming aware of the three-part cycle of the breath. Then, when you can do so without distraction, move on to *qualifying* the three parts of the breath.

On each careful mindful inhalation, consciously know that you are breathing in positive energy i.e. peace, joy, gratitude etc. along with life-giving oxygen. You may imagine, and mindfully see, this energy entering your body in the form of a bright *white light*. The positive energies you inhale increase the mindfulness of feeling deeply inspired at the end of each inhalation. This is *qualified inhalation*.

On each careful mindful retention, consciously know that the positive energies you have inhaled are now transported and distributed inside your entire body, rejuvenating each cell in your internal organs, muscles, joints and so on. See this mindfully as a radiant *red light* dissolving blockages in the body and rejuvenating your energy. This red radiation arouses a warm feeling that spreads and abides throughout your whole body including the coarse and subtle channels. This is *qualified retention*.

On each careful exhalation, consciously know that the out-going breath takes away negative energies in your body, including any illness, discomfort and negative thoughts or emotions. Let these negative energies flow out of your body along with the carbon dioxide you exhale. As you do so, see mindfully that this negative energy leaves your body as a *blue light*, or in the form of dark and dense energy. Once it has left your body, the negative energy dissipates, losing its effect on you. Mindfully feel that you are lighter and peaceful. This is *qualified exhalation*.

This triad of identifying the three distinct phases of each round of breath, ascribing the three qualities, and visualising the three colours is referred to here as *Qualified Rounds of Breathing*.

Continue to maintain your attention by seeing these three phases in each round of breath. Try to do six or seven rounds, or a few minutes, of Qualified Rounds of Breath for each uninterrupted bout of attentive effort.

It is important that you try to recognise the quality of each of the three phases of each round of the breath as you concentrate. If you become distracted by external sensory objects, such as sights, sounds or smells, try to gently bring your focus back to the breath. Similarly, if your concentration is interrupted by thoughts, simply return your attention to the breath. In this practice, it is important not to push away your thoughts or reject them. You should also avoid following any distracting thoughts, or being swept up in a `conversation' with yourself Merely note your thoughts arising and bring your attention back to the mindfulness of your breath.

After every bout of effort of Qualified Rounds of Breath then learn to take a *mini-break*, even if you are not distracted. Learn also to take mini breaks when your clarity is good as well as when your clarity is poor. Skilfully use your concerted effort in short, sharp bouts of effort and be realistic in regards to your attention span.

If your meditation is endowed with the attributes of *doing*, *knowing*, *seeing* and *feeling* and you are making use of the *mini-breaks,* you will be able to break the back of any distraction or discouragement and avoid the dangers of getting attached to any particular flavour in your meditation. Do not get attached to the frothy surface of the cappuccino!

To complete your meditation session simply reverse the order with which it was begun. From the Qualified Rounds of Breath, gently bring your mind back to just noting the three cycles of breath. After a few moments of noting these three cycles, review the elements of your posture in reverse order: the serene gaze of the eyes, the relaxed mouth and jaw, the neck slightly bent forward, the balanced and relaxed arms and shoulders, the straight back, the joined hands in your lap, and the solid base formed by your crossed legs and your bottom. Feel the earth beneath you and the presence of any other objects in your meditation space. As you rise from your meditation, try to retain your more relaxed state of mind.

By following the breath we are following something that is constantly changing and we are sharpening our ability to remain present when the mind is restless. We are acting as a private detective to negative thoughts and afflictions as they arise. The breath is a reference point to see where one's mind is. When you are not paying attention to the object, you would not know if you are focused or not. Recognising the patterns, we see how and from where our thoughts and attitudes arise and we will now be apprehending the cause of suffering just as the Buddha taught.

If you began your meditation session with the right preparation, having developed the right motivation for the practice, and if you followed these instructions, you may now feel lighter, more relaxed and more centred. After your meditation, dedicate the benefits of your practice both to yourself and to those with whom you relate. You might dedicate your practice for all beings in order that they will attain the same state of calmness and serenity that you are trying to cultivate.

Pain in Meditation

Pain is inevitable, suffering is optional!

Lama Choedak Rinpoche

Craving is the root cause of all suffering. The Buddha taught the *Noble Truth* of Suffering, not the *Demon* of Suffering. Whether you meditate or whether you lie on the beach, the unsatisfactory nature of life is inevitable. In meditation, we soon encounter the craving not to experience discomfort in the sitting. Almost everyone knows that there is *no pain, no gain* in worthwhile endeavours. One thing you can learn to do is to elevate pain to the level of the teacher. Often the most difficult situations are the ones that bring out the best in us.

Aches and pains in the body are quite a natural process. Even lying in bed there is discomfort. Many of the questions that arise in meditation relate to pain. Pain is an expression of our rigidity, an object to be despised and avoided. We have a very rigid mental posture towards pain - we don't like it! All the physical cushions can only help so much but it is the mental cushions that are the teachings and instructions that we really need.

You need to remain calm and work with the pain. When you fear and despise pain, the more it will hurt. It is important to remember that meditation is not a suppression technique. It is not a desensitiser but rather it increases your awareness of the pain. You can change the whole strategy of your meditation from one of despising pain to one of examining its impermanent nature.

In the beginning do not deny and despise the pain. As soon as you begin to register pain then you will recognise it as something that is arising. It is good to deal with a fire while the flame is small. You can use the Qualified Rounds of Breathing, described in the previous chapter, to reach the pain. Imagine yourself sending positive white and red light to those areas that are calling out for it. When the pain is in the lower part of the body, fill up the body with the qualities of the white and red lights in the Qualified Rounds of Breathings and allow the pain to float up to the surface. This will prevent the pain from becoming localised by using the circulatory nature of the breathing to bring it up and then exhale it.

Remember that pain is temporary. Give the mind a choice of what it has to do with the body and try not to be persuaded that the pain is too much for you. Become dispassionate towards the pain by creating a space between yourself and the body; subject and object. See the pain as something that the body has and see that the pain is not you. Perhaps you need to move the body slightly - it might even be only a mental shift.

Understand it is not the meditation that is the cause of the pain. It is the nature of existence that is causing the pain, just as fire has the nature of burning. Reflect that one's own pain is minuscule in relation to the pain of the whole world. Take the responsibility for the pain you have caused in the past, by imagining that the meditation is a gentle but necessary kind of healing medical procedure.

Meditation on Pain

Pain will bring me onto the path of cultivating inner strength. It will teach me the skills to accept and to see how it rises and falls.

While paying it my full attention, I will whisper of its rise and its fall; otherwise it may be heard as a loud scream from the outside.

Seeing the rise of pain will show me how to search for methods to heal and to realise that running away only deepens the pain.

By knowing its transient nature I will find the space to flow and spread and to find the wisdom to nurture and nurse the part of me that is in pain.

Pain humbles my arrogance and crumbles my attachment to health. It reminds me of the fragility of the body, and it purifies my negativities.

As the trial and test of life, pain evokes hidden wisdom, and, as a timely reminder, it says "pain is prevalent".

Observing my own pain opens my heart in a compassionate way and I experience a burst of compassion towards others with more pain than me.

Seeing how trivial my own pain is, I become patient with myself.
I find strength in tolerance and acceptance, rather than in
rejecting the pain.

I feel gratitude to those who care for me as a loved one.
Day after day they attend many patients like myself.
Thinking of their dedication soothes my pain.

If I can skilfully deal with my own pain, I will gain the strength
to overcome it. Let my pain radiate rays of goodwill and peace to
illuminate the darkness of sorrow and ignorance.

Obstacles and their Antidotes - Part I

The remedies are the understanding of the obstacles.

Lama Choedak Rinpoche

It is natural for us to face obstacles whenever we try to achieve anything worthwhile in our lives. The practice of meditation is no exception. However, the obstacles to meditation are difficult to identify.

When learning to meditate, we recognise that we have been habitually seeing difficulties in life as a pain in the neck. *Obstacles* and their *antidotes* present a new kind of positive mental language that we can begin to cultivate in meditation. It is not about remedying obstacles to the point of trying to get rid of them but rather about learning from them and adjusting your application of the remedies.

Meditation is a powerful tool to increase one's awareness. Like the scientist who examines the pathogen under stringent laboratory conditions in order to understand it's nature, the strict form employed in the discipline of meditation provides one with the right conditions to accurately identify the obstacles.

Traditionally, there are said to be five obstacles and eight antidotes. In this section we will discuss the first and second obstacles - laziness and forgetfulness. The remaining three obstacles, which are the domain of the more experienced meditator, will be discussed later in the handbook.

Laziness - The First Obstacle

This is an obstacle we face in everything virtuous we attempt in our lives. It can arise in cleverly disguised and convincing forms that prevent us from even beginning to meditate.

Laziness is described in several recognisable forms, including -

- being easily discouraged to the point that our motivation collapses,
- excessive attachment to comfort,
- unrealistic expectations, or,
- completely occupying oneself with futile activities.

This first obstacle has more antidotes than any of the others. The four antidotes to laziness are - faith, determination, joyous effort and pliancy.

> **Faith** - It is not difficult to appreciate how improving one's ability to concentrate single-pointedly on a positive, wholesome object in meditation can benefit our mental and physical well-being. There is a lot of empirical scientific research these days to support this. We don't need some kind of religious devotion to have faith in meditation, one only has to be aware of the benefits of practicing it.
>
> Having this kind of *lucid* faith in knowing the goodness of meditation has to be followed by *aspiring* faith. Aspiring faith is a strong form of positive wanting to meditate and what is needed make it to the cushion. We will be stimulating our enthusiasm in whatever way we can, through listening to and reading instructions on how to do the actual meditation. We might join a formal class or meditation group.

With time, we experience the fruits of our aspirations and efforts. This is a consolidation of a stronger conviction that has now reaped the benefits through one's endeavours. We acquire a genuine sense of peace and happiness in our life. There is less tendency to find excuses not to meditate. There is a sense of trust in the goodness of meditation. One is now in possession of *trustworthy* faith to do and maintain our meditation practice.

Determination - Whether we desire simple peace of mind in our daily life or the ultimate enlightenment of Buddha, it all depends on the degree of our wholeheartedness and perseverance. There is no skill or quality that does not come about without this determination. We need to familiarise ourselves with the teachings on *impermanence* and the precious opportunity that these present life circumstances offer, in order to develop the determination to meditate. Determination to attend a meditation course or a short group meditation retreat can give you a lot of confidence and empower you with a life skill and an experience of true peace and happiness.

Joyous Effort – The faith and determination should be genuine and not a form of obligation. We should do everything with joy and gratitude and meditation is no exception. With an understanding of the *Law of Cause and Effect*, we are joyous in knowing that only good can come from Right Effort and a good discipline to meditate. The physician's medicine might be a little bitter to swallow but in comparison to the pains that we are alleviating, we happily forebear small displeasures. Long term benefits are the hardest to win, but are the most meaningful and bring the greatest sense of satisfaction. We are now possessed with insight that enthusiastically invests effort in meditation.

Pliancy – With the implementation of the first three antidotes, it is possible that one no longer experiences gross obstacles either physically or mentally in the same way as before. One's physical body is no longer an obstacle but it has transformed into a useful tool that is readily serviceable. There is no longing for anything and one does not need to seek calmness or peace from outside. One is not rocked by the roller-coaster of Samsara as before and one's mind is easily made happy. In combating laziness, therefore, pliancy is more of an effect of the previous three antidotes.

Pliancy is an indication that the meditator is healing through meditation. The mind has been made beautiful and useful - this brings a lasting sense of peace and calm. The mind does not hold onto hate and negative emotions. This appeals to the meditator. It is noticeable how flexible one's mind has become and how able it is to change and be liberated from the past. One's mind is open and one can see the infinite choices that are available to us.

Take advantage of this human boat
Free yourself from sorrow's mighty stream
This vessel will later be hard to find
The time that you have now, you fool, is not for sleep.

Shantideva

(Refer to the analytical meditations and classical readings at the back of this booklet for more about the obstacle of Laziness and its antidotes).

Forgetfulness - The Second Obstacle

This obstacle is experienced by those who have already engaged in meditation and have received some instructions, but cannot recall all the details of the instruction in doing the meditation. One may be sitting on the cushion but there is no active engagement, even in keeping the correct posture, let alone being able to watch the Qualified Rounds of Breath. Much time is spent sitting, but forgetting what, why and how to do the meditation properly.

Forgetfulness signals a weakness in motivation and a slackness in recollecting and applying the instructions of the meditation practice. When training in any skill, trade, craft or hobby, we meet this obstacle while we are learning the *what for*, the *how to* and the *why*.

The antidote, therefore, to this obstacle is mindfulness.

> **Mindfulness** - This is something that we are familiar with but in the context of this obstacle, it is a question of where we are choosing to orientate our attention. The structure of the meditation is important to remedying forgetfulness. Prepare all the necessary requirements before beginning the session, such as a suitable place to sit, a comfortable cushion, etc.
>
> Having attended to your environment, familiarise yourself with the body posture and its significance before you proceed to watching the Qualified Round of Breath. Try to have a clear picture of the instructions that teach you how to deal with repeated distractions as well as forgetfulness. Within the meditation, look for the four attributes of doing, knowing, seeing and feeling when scanning your posture or watching the Qualified Round of Breath.
>
> Attend teachings on meditation and associate with other meditators to help deepen your level of understanding. Do not forget to have the right

motivation at the start of your sessions, which in itself will enhance your knowledge of the practice and its benefits. You should not engage in meditation with the wrong motivation. Do not conclude a meditation session in a hurry, or in a state of extreme emotional distress.

Once you have developed mindfulness, then all the antidotes will appear as they are required; forgetfulness will not become a problem. Just as one is constantly mindful of food and drink when one is hungry and thirsty, when we have mastered the practice of mindfulness, we will be mindful of the obstacles to our meditation practice and their antidotes.

MINDFULNESS OF SPEECH

Pause for a cause.

Lama Choedak Rinpoche

Mindfulness of Speech is an extension of Mindfulness of Feeling and is a product of formal meditation training. One is now learning to pragmatically apply the fruits of formal sitting meditation in everyday life situations. In meditation, we see how words and phrases comprise one's thoughts. Speech comes from the neurolinguistic processes that have already been formed in our thought patterns. Thought is usually the forerunner of all our experiences and actions.

Through the practice of Mindfulness of Speech, we see the intent that gives rise to our speech. The ambience of one's overall mindfulness is generally enhanced. The meditator is assisted in being more selective as to which thoughts will be entertained. All problems start with an undetected negative thought.

Calm Abiding Meditation is practised in order to arouse compassion. Our meditation is the actualising of the prayers that we have recited that *all beings may be happy and be free from the cause of suffering*. A person who has a sense of sacredness and dignity within himself is not offend-able by the unskilful and absentminded use of speech by another. They have established for themselves a boundary which cannot be crossed, like the javelin thrower.

The decision not to retaliate is not a religiously motivated puritanical one. Refraining from retaliation is not some heavy burden that is done out of a sense of weakness disempowerment. We pause

41

to avoid causing suffering. So much suffering is generated through talking, as if one is complaining about a fire while at the same time throwing fuel on it. It is a safety practice, a refuge.

Many things are said mindlessly as if there are no consequences. Many sufferings in the community are created by bad mouthing others. A person who meditates will become aware of how to use speech. Many years of good deeds can be destroyed by idle gossip and slanderous language. People become so driven in slandering others, and saying many negative things without checking the facts. They become so inspired to spread rumour as if they will thus save the world. The negative effect of slandering others is bad body odour and mouth and throat related illness.

Meditation on Blessing One's Speech

The best time for this practice is early in the morning before speaking -

In the centre of my tongue appears an orange seed syllable DHIH
The seed syllable of Manjushri, the Bodhisattva of Wisdom.
Representing the speech making energy of the Enlightened Ones,
The syllable streams out many light rays to illuminate my body.

Striking all animate and inanimate phenomenon in this and other
universes, the light rays gather infinite positive qualities.
Absorbing into the seed syllable, it melts and transforms
Into a cool, refreshing and soothing stream of nectar.

Just as the morning sunrise dispels the darkness, the orange
translucent stream of nectar removes the negative verbal habitual
patterns and blesses my speech to become gentle, soft and truthful.

Wherever the nectar flows, it implants the seed of mindfulness,
Giving the power to control the use of my own speech and the
wisdom not to be adversely affected by other people's verbal abuse
by understanding them as expressions of their mental anguish.

When other people are unable to use their speech skilfully
May I develop an empathy to remain calm, focused and patient
So that they will be relieved from their mental anguish
By the blessing of Manjushri, the Lord of Speech.

Let this recitation of the sacred mantra of Manjushri
Guard my own speech throughout all times
And may I receive the blessings upon my tongue
Just as snow flakes falling on a warm rock.

Mantra of Manjushri

OM A RA PA TSA NA DHIH ༀ་ཨ་ར་པ་ཙ་ན་ཧྲཱིཿ

(After reciting the mantra at least 21 times, finish with a deep breath and recite the last syllable DHIH as many times as possible in one breath, and then swallow)

Everyday Mindfulness

One who is heedful is happy and one who is not is not.

Nagarjuna

Mindfulness is important in all occasions and it benefits ourselves and others. In recent years psychologists have come to appreciate the importance of understanding the mind. Mind has always been since time immemorial. Mind is the oldest subject, we are always using mindfulness though it is not always consciously present.

The cause of mindfulness is calmness. We have to be calm to distinguish between the perception and the perceived. There should be an absence of turbulence. Calmness is the conscious act of pacifying the mind of certain negative thoughts, feelings and emotions. When we are calm we become careful of what information we receive. When we are not calm then our response will not be carefully thought through. When we are agitated by negativity then there is only one response that you will fire on the spot. When we are careful we will begin to have more ability to pick the best response from several choices.

When chopping wood with mindfulness we will not only see the wood but also know how to hold the axe carefully. We may hold the handle so tightly that we may cause a blister. If we held the handle too loosely we might drop the axe. We need to find a middle way. Using mindfulness we are able to look, and at the same time see. We will see the purpose for which the mindfulness is directed. We only learn the skilful method by knowing the danger of the two extremes. Look, see, learn and change. Change is finding a new method of holding the axe.

There are a lot of instances in life where we have been holding on too tightly or too loosely. Seeing is recognising the things that we did in the past that were too fundamentalist or too controlling, and that needed to be relaxed. Seeing empowers us not to repeat the past error. We learn from past experiences and then we begin to change.

We practice mindfulness only in the present moment. We do not have to practice it all day. Mindfulness is full precision in the present, not fast forwarding to the future or playing back the past. When we are not calm we are agitated by the past or worried about the future.

Mindfulness might be forgetting the other things that would otherwise take the mind away to become totally distracted. Things are done wholeheartedly as if the rest of the world does not exist, without being distracted and with undivided attention. Things are done more quickly and accurately. You can foresee how the long term benefits will be great.

The effect of the mindfulness of good intentions will be revealed by the result. Sincerely doing something will have the power to sustain your confidence and concentration. When you are careful, then you will discover the love and meaning of the effort. Mindfulness boosts optimism and will transform the situation. Meditation blesses us so that we are able to see the good that comes from others and our actions are empowered by that.

With mindfulness we see the positive and the good in the intention of other people. Now you are beginning to read the heart of others. You are not worried by a few poorly delivered words and you will distil the essence and perceive the wholeness in others.

One sesame seed contains only a little oil but many sesame seeds yield a lot of oil. Even though it may not seem like much on it's own, we can learn to do everything with mindfulness and faith to ensure a beneficial outcome. It is better to do fewer things with better quality. We will not become exhausted and there will be more happiness and greater effect.

Doing something motivated by a feeling of obligation but without our heart being properly involved, can be very taxing and tiring.

You could be pretending you are calm but there is resentment and passive aggression. Mindfulness in our work is very relevant, and meditation can help to recondition our motivation in our daily work. If we don't then we won't serve people or the job or ourselves very well. This kind of mindfulness is primarily directed towards our own happiness.

Walking and Standing

Buddha taught that the mindfulness practice should be applied to all activities including sitting, standing, walking and lying down. Walking meditation with mindfulness is a very pleasant experience, even for beginners. People walk for some time every day but often with their mind full of busy thoughts. One may be unable to sit for long, due to health problems or physical limitations. It is important to know how to stay calm and meditative in other physical activities.

Slow and peaceful walking meditation can be done in relation to the mindfulness of watching the round of breath. First, one should stand still for few minutes before doing the walking meditation. Resolve to walk mindfully, a symbol that one is following in the footsteps of the Buddha. While being aware of the positive energy of the ground in front, inhale mindfully and lift the left foot in the air. Retain the breath while the foot reaches it highest point and glides forward, and then mindfully exhale as the foot descends and touches the ground. Perhaps walking barefoot could enhance the mindful sensation of the foot lifting, stretching and touching the ground.

Additionally, each time the foot is lifted you can mentally recite OM, when the foot glides forward mentally recited AH, and when the foot descends and touches the ground mentally mentally recite HUM. You might walk around a holy object, temple, stupa or a peace garden. A Buddhist always walks clockwise around such objects.

You can use a mala to count the steps and maintain a gentle pace of walking to remedy distraction. Don't forget the mini-breaks!

Walking and sitting meditation might be alternated for thirty minutes each. Include a few minutes in between chanting some prayers such as Four Immeasurables or the Shakyamuni Buddha Mantra. In this way one can learn to walk mindfully.

When doing standing meditation, it is important to keep the spine straight with relaxed arms falling either side of the body and the neck maintaining the same position as in the sitting posture. While standing with conscious awareness, keep the posture, then do the Qualified Rounds of Breathing exactly as one does in the sitting posture. One can do standing meditation for ten minutes after a thirty minute sitting, followed by 30 minutes of walking meditation.

OBSTACLES AND THEIR ANTIDOTES - PART II

*The way a person deals with pain and distraction
during Calm Abiding Meditation reveals a lot about
the way they deal with their deluded perceptions.*

Lama Choedak Rinpoche

Dullness and Agitation - The Third Obstacle

These obstacles occur only when one has already developed the habit of meditating regularly. By this stage, one has overcome the problem of bodily aches and pains.

Having become familiar with the practice of focussing on the object of meditation, one now encounters dullness. Dullness brings with it a loss of clarity and spaciousness and there is a kind of heaviness. The mind's mode of apprehending disappears and there is a withdrawal of the mind within itself, away from the object of meditation. This is a form of internal distraction which could even be mistaken for meditation due to a false sense of stability. This stage is tricky because the meditator has become encouraged by the lack of external distractions, but they have arrived at a state of mental stagnation.

Dullness means an absence of knowing. It is only symbolic of the gross dull abiding in life. Dullness is the fundamental sign of ignorance and combating it in meditation is the direct remedy to the gross and subtle afflictions that dominates our daily patterns.

Subtle dullness is even harder to detect. This develops when one has succeeded in developing mental stability with a degree of clarity but insufficient intensity. This is a state which is most commonly mistaken for true Calm Abiding. This particular obstacle indicates that there are still subtle elements of laziness creeping in, even though gross drowsiness and lethargy are no longer occurring.

Gross agitation is the excited mind involuntarily going in search of external objects. Whether it seeks virtuous thoughts or not, this should be stopped during Calm Abiding Meditation as it distracts us from our purpose of resting the mind on the object of meditation.

Subtle agitation is a little harder to detect. This is said to occur when the mind does not even notice that part of the attention has gone out to an external object, while at the same time it is resting on the object of meditation.

Dullness and agitation, are thus increasingly more subtle and stay with the meditator for a very long time.

Dullness and agitation arise because of the lack of balance in the intensity of the meditator's effort. The antidote to both dullness and agitation is **introspection** which scrutinises the quality of one's mindfulness. Like fine tuning a guitar, it requires the experience of one who has developed his ear in playing the instrument. The great Indian master Chandragomin once said, "When I develop effort, mental excitement occurs, but when I remedy that, mental sinking sets in." Be aware that it is necessary to exercise great force of attention to remedy this problem.

Sloppy arrangement of the sessions could be contributing to dullness. If you find that you are unable to avoid subtle dullness by applying the antidote of introspection, you can stop the session and reflect on topics such as the benefits of meditation, the qualities of the Buddha, and the fortunate condition of your precious human rebirth. These reflections can brighten the mind. (also see *Developing the Motivation to Meditate* at the back of this handbook) It is good to do this while taking a walk, preferably in cool surroundings. If possible, do this in a high place with a view of a valley and an expansive sky.

Alternatively, wash your face or even your body with cold water and open some doors and windows to let a cool breeze into the room. Recognising that dullness is present immediately clarifies the mind of the meditator. Once you feel wide awake, you can resume your meditation in a brighter and happier mood.

The problem of agitation may be remedied by reflecting upon the difficulties and sufferings that exist in the world in order to depress or sober the mind. (see *Meditation on Death and Impermanence* at the back of this handbook) There is no real happiness in this world because nothing lasts. We all have to die one day, and leave our nearest and dearest ones. We have no choice about this. No-one is a reliable friend, as everyone is selfish. Neither wealth nor power can produce happiness. They only create more anxiety and frustration.

Another useful technique to remedy agitation is to temporarily reduce the length of the meditation sessions. Mini-breaks are especially effective to remedy this obstacle.

Learning to do Super Qualified Rounds of Breathing is a key to improving introspection. Mindfulness of Breathing is enhanced by learning to see the gentle beginning, the full peak and the gentle conclusion of each of the three phases of the breath - the inhalation, retention and exhalation. Thus, we are now distinguishing nine sub-segments in each Super Qualified Round of Breath. One will eventually be able to apply mindfulness by doing, knowing, seeing and feeling each sub-segment of Super Qualified Rounds of Breathing as they occur in real time. The effect is to gain an excellent degree of resolution and clarity with a balance of intensity that is devoid of the faults of subtle dullness and agitation.

Non-application of the Antidotes

This problem is related to the third obstacle of dullness and agitation. If one fails to recognise the obstacles through mindfulness and introspection, one will not know how and when to apply the antidotes appropriately. One must therefore ensure that one is fully familiar with the nature of all the possible obstacles that may occur during meditation, and that one knows the exact antidotes to apply to each obstacles when it arises.

Over-application of the Antidotes

When the antidotes to the third obstacle of dullness and agitation are applied, one could slip into the habit of using them too often even when they are not needed. It is therefore a fault to use antidotes when there are no obstacles present. The forceful attention should be interrupted or relaxed but not totally, as there is the danger of a re-occurrence of the third obstacle. The solution to this problem is careful application of antidotes. They should be applied evenly and only when necessary.

Summing Up the Importance of the Obstacles and Antidotes

There is a meaning that we can bring to the obstacles in meditation. We begin to see the very nature of the obstacles when we confront them and elevate them the status of teacher. We develop respect towards the obstacle and we now have a partner towards which we have softened.

Afflictions, by definition, are difficult to detect but during the meditation one is sharp and alert enough to analyse the obstacles. One will not be intimidated by the causes of pain from the past, when we know how they arose and when we have stopped creating them.

Progress is inherent when we are confronted with adversarial factors, and then learn from them. There is no inherently existing strength but rather, the conquerer has come to know the strategies of the opposition very well. We are not intimidated by the opponent but are curious about its new tricks. There is a kind of great hearted attitude that is born. We are not losing towards the obstacles and pain, and discursive thoughts are not the cause of further problems.

Good meditators experience tiredness, but because there is no gross craving present, they will not be excessively depleted by such an experience. Good practitioners are able to sleep less because that attachment has been eased. When the mind is less inclined materially it is not weighed down by such tiredness. Generally speaking, whatever is on our mind is what will affect our experience. The meditator has the ability not to sit in that thought long enough to be drowned.

Five Experiences of
Calm Abiding Meditation

1. Experience of Recognition of the Thoughts

As one tries to focus the mind on the object of meditation, a continuous thought stream arises which could not be anticipated by one's gross mind. Actually, the mind is burdened with such thoughts all the time, but because the effort was not previously made to closely place the mind in meditation, one was unable to notice them. Not knowing this to be so, the meditator may become discouraged to notice so many thoughts disturbing one's meditation. This, however, is the first and most important experience of Calm Abiding Meditation, known as *Experience of Recognition of the Thoughts*. It is said to be like watching water fall off a steep mountain.

2. Experience of the Resting of the Thoughts

As one repeatedly places the mind on the object of meditation while being aware of the rising thoughts, after some time one's thoughts become reluctant to arise. However, they do not cease completely. Just as the meditator notices the slowing pace of his thoughts, the pace will start to speed up again. As one becomes more aware of this process, it in turn will cease to arise. This alternative repetition of the rising, slowing and ceasing procession of thoughts is the second experience of Calm Abiding Meditation, known as *Experience of the Resting of the Thoughts*. It is akin to a creek making its way through a steep and narrow gorge.

3. Experience of the Exhaustion of the Thoughts

As the meditator becomes familiar with the alternating rising and ceasing of his own thoughts and as one continues to study this process, the thoughts will miraculously disappear. As one attempt to maintain this state, new thoughts however will burst in to interrupt the clarity, and then remain, but in a state of sudden exhaustion. This is the third experience of Calm Abiding Meditation, known as the *Experience of the Exhaustion of the Thoughts*. It is similar to the sight of a pool, into which streams from three different valleys converge at intervals.

4. Experience of the Ocean With Waves

At this stage, with the help of this new awareness, the meditator develops a state of calmness and stability. One remains stable for a good length of time without experiencing any obstacles. One will have the control to direct the mind with little effort to remain attentively focussed. One or two thoughts may arise which will again naturally die off. This is the fourth experience of Calm Abiding Meditation known as the *Experience of the Ocean with Waves*. It is similar to watching waves breaking over a peaceful ocean.

5. Experience of Ocean Without Waves

This is the stage where the meditator does not require any effort to focus the mind on a chosen object of meditation. There are no external sensory objects nor any inner thoughts causing mental discursiveness. This is the fifth experience of Calm Abiding Meditation known as the *Experience of Ocean without Waves*. It is like a peaceful ocean without any waves.

The stability, clarity and intensity of the meditation may make the ocean of the mind appear clear, seeing all the grains of sand at the bottom. It has become clear that all knowable phenomena are not what they appear. The insight of seeing *no-self* can only dawn through proper Calm Abiding Meditation, not otherwise. Intellectual understanding of the doctrine of emptiness without the discipline of doing Calm Abiding Meditation may cause more waves of discursive thoughts than it calms.

NINE MENTAL STAGES OF CALM ABIDING MEDITATION

Holding the rope of mindfulness and the hook of alertness,
May I resolve to tame this mind, which is like a wild elephant.
Steadily focusing the mind with a moderate application of antidotes,
May I discover what causes its restlessness.

Lama Choedak Rinpoche

The point of departure for Calm Abiding Meditation is concentration on a single object. Whether this is an image of the Buddha, a seed syllable or the flow of the breath makes no difference. The average person passes his days allowing himself to be swept hither and thither by an infinity of disparate thoughts that are, as it were, external to himself. The immediate result of one pointed concentration on an object is prompt and lucid censorship of all distractions that dominate, or constitute profane consciousness. The practice of Calm Abiding Meditation enables us to control the two generators of mental fluidity: sense activity and the activity of the subconscious. Mind control is the ability to intervene directly, and at will, in the functioning of these two mental whirlwinds.

The Nine Stages of Calm Abiding Meditation are difficult to explain or understand until a practitioner has direct experience of these stages himself by doing consistent and prolonged meditation practice. The symbolic diagram of Taming the Elephant Mind has been used in the Tibetan Buddhist tradition as a teaching aid for several hundred years. It is a common feature of temple murals in Tibet, where deep meditation practice is taught. Due to the subjective and experiential meaning encoded in this highly intelligent pictographic message, Taming the Elephant Mind has never been an easy illustration to popularise as, for example, the Wheel of Life has been. Only through prolonged meditation retreat will one understand its value, by understanding the central Buddhist doctrine of how to trace the source of past difficulties back to ones' own mind.

In general, the metaphor of the elephant is widely used in Buddhist texts. In certain Buddhist Scriptures, the elephant is used to symbolise strength and endurance. It is an object of reverence. Many villagers in South East Asia believe the elephant is sacred and is to be treated as a symbol of purity.

In Mahayana Buddhism, the elephant is one of the *Seven Attributes of a Universal Monarch*. Perhaps, in this context, the elephant in an illustration depicts the fact that the mind represents the substratum of all experiences, a concept central to the Buddhist doctrine of enlightenment.

As far as I am aware, there is no scriptural description of this important illustration, with the exception of one verse by the Buddha, in which he states that the elephant mind has to be tamed by using the *rope of mindfulness and hook of alertness*. Both Shantideva's Bodhisattvacaryavatara and Kamalashila's Bhavanakrama highlight this idea, but do not go into any detail. The drawing is definitely much later than these two works, but is probably inspired by them. It appears to be a creation of a Tibetan named Naljorpa who must have spent prolonged periods in retreat and experienced the Nine Stages himself.

As in the Zen Ox-herding Tradition, depicting the mind as a wild elephant may seem daunting to beginners. However, because of the undoubted usefulness of this illustration in explaining the various subtle meditative states, I have compiled the following description of Taming the Elephant Mind to complement the preceding notes in this handbook. It is based on the oral transmission and deeply felt experiences of the Calm Abiding Meditation practice, and the realisation of the significance of sacred symbols in Tibetan Buddhist meditation training.

If the mind is not tamed, it will bring many more sufferings than a rampaging wild elephant. The elephant may cause damage to others, but the unruly mind causes self destruction. Discovering that there is an unruly mind that can be tamed is a healthy discovery. One can then learn how to prevent destruction caused by such an untamed mind.

We have been wasting our time in searching outside for the cause of our unhappiness, when in fact it originates from within our own minds. It is important not to kill or suppress the elephant, (our mind) but to tame it steadily without losing sight of the immense value of its formidable power. A good elephant trainer tames the elephant by learning about it and making it to do as he orders, i.e. to carry heavy loads and so forth. A person who understands the nature of his mind and its potential will do likewise. He does not become a slave to his deluded mind, but instead awakens himself from the slumber of dullness.

The detailed description follows the diagram from bottom to top.

1. Orientation

The monk standing at the beginning of the path (at the bottom right of the illustration) symbolises the beginning of the meditator's spiritual journey through Calm Abiding Meditation. More elaborate diagrams show the monk with his back to a house, indicating his renunciation of the home of unsatisfactory worldly existence.

Holding (a) a hook and (b) a rope in his hands indicates that the monk must have received detailed instructions on the practice. To begin trying to find the object of meditation, a student needs to have received some direction and guidance in order to understand the aim of meditation. Hearing instructions from the mouth of a teacher on the practice will empower a disciple through the transmission of knowledge.

The elephant's gait and darkness indicate the state of wildness of the mind. The dark, running elephant symbolises the habituated dull mind and the enthusiastic dark monkey represents the agitated nature of an untamed mind. The monkey has the elephant on a leash and is luring the dull elephant, encouraging it to follow its old habitual inclinations.

Holding the hook of introspection towards the dull and restless mind is the first stage of placing and orientating the mind towards the object of meditation.

2. Repeated Orientation

On the left side of the first bend at the bottom of the path, the meditator has tied his upper robe around his waist to indicate his determination to tame the mind. The white patches already appearing on the elephant and monkey's heads symbolise that at this stage, by exerting effort, the meditator is starting to gain some degree of confidence and can remain stable in spite of numerous distractions.

The (c) flames along the side of the path indicate that effort is required to focus on the object of meditation when any of the five distractive sensory objects manifest. The size of the flame indicates the degree of the effort that is exerted.

The five sensory objects are represented by (d) silk cloth for touch, (e) fruit for taste, (f) cymbals for sound, (g) conch-shell (filled with perfume) for smell, and (h) mirror for sight. They also symbolise the five obstacles of Calm Abiding Meditation. The order in which the sensory objects are placed along the path indicate the relative gross to subtle nature of each sense object. For example, even if the meditator is able to focus his mind on the object of meditation, the first pressing problem is generally associated with touch, i.e. physical pain and discomfort.

3. Repaired Orientation

At the third stage, the monk has lassoed the elephant with the rope of mindfulness in his right hand, while retaining the hook of introspection in his left hand. This indicates that the meditator has matured considerably and has acquired the skill to alternate the use of these two tools.

Consequently, he has discovered the nature of distraction as being neither external nor inherently existent. This is beautifully illustrated by the backward glance of the elephant. The recognition of distraction in the meditator's unsettled mind should not be confused with finding an inherent distracting object.

Recognition of the cause of distraction also enables the meditator to discover more subtle dullness, illustrated here by the sudden appearance of a hare mounted on the elephant's back. The subtle dullness is generally explained as water under ice, but here it may be better understood if one considers the animal's character and the destruction it can cause to the land.

The backward glance of the monkey symbolises the restless mind that has become somewhat subdued.

4. Closer Orientation

Stages 3 and 4 are similar, in that the agitated monkey has lost the attention of the elephant. The monk can maintain his concentration through mindfulness alone without exerting the application of introspection. This is indicated by the monk not having to hold or poke the hook to the elephant. The shift in the monk's use of these two tools indicates the correct use of the antidotes to remedy the obstacles. By lassoing the elephant the rope is functioning to sustain mindfulness.

The roles of the monkey and elephant are now completely reversed, which is indicated by the monkey having to glance back at the elephant. The increased whiteness of the three animals indicates greater familiarity with the nature of one's own mind has been achieved through closer placement of the mind on the object of meditation.

5. Subdued Orientation

At this stage, the monk has managed to considerably subdue the gross aspects of the obstacles of dullness and agitation. Touching the hook on the elephant's nose indicates the importance of self encouragement.

The monk's relationship with the object of meditation has made a complete shift. The monkey following the elephant indicates that by not rejecting discursive thoughts, the experienced meditator has fully realised the ability to utilise the obstacles to improve his meditation.

6. Pacified Orientation

By the sixth stage, the meditator has fully overcome all gross obstacles. The disappearance of the hare indicates that from here onwards, the meditator will not suffer from subtle dullness either. He no longer needs to constantly use the tools on the elephant and monkey, and the flames of the effort required in meditation are beginning to decrease.

The physical body will present no obstacle whatsoever as indicated by the elephant and monkey's obedience to the meditator. Nonetheless, the meditator continues to sustain and refine his mindfulness and introspection, as shown by the conscientious manner in which he is holding onto the hook and rope.

7. Thoroughly Pacified Orientation

At the seventh stage, the meditator has abandoned the conventional use of the two tools, the remedies to the obstacles. This indicates the realisation that his mind is intrinsically calm and serene. There is now no need to use any external device.

When one reaches this level, one neither requires a peaceful place to meditate, nor perceives any antithesis to peace. The subtle residues of discursive thoughts are indicated by the monkey's pleading with the meditator not to abandon him. The meditator's confidence is represented by his ability to stand between the monkey and the elephant. The posture of the meditator expresses his equanimity.

8. One Pointed Concentration

At the eighth stage of Calm Abiding Meditation, the elephant has become completely white, which indicates the removal of all traces of subtle dullness and agitation. Also, the disappearance of the monkey, and the monk politely showing the elephant the way with his hand, expresses immense confidence that the elephant will now be able to abide effortlessly and one-pointedly without interruption.

9. Equally Abiding

The ninth and final stage of Calm Abiding is *equilibrium*, a state of mind which is the actual attainment of Calm Abiding Meditation. The meditator seated in the cross legged posture, with the elephant beside him (i), indicates that the meditator is now practicing uninterrupted and effortless Calm Abiding meditation. One of the significant signs of attaining Calm Abiding is the development of a rapturous feeling in the body. As a result, one will not suffer from gross physical pain.

The flying monk (j), indicates the weightlessness of the body which signifies physical pliancy. The monk riding on the elephant (k) symbolises mental bliss and mental pliancy, arising from complete subjugation of mental afflictions.

The sword in the meditator's right hand symbolises his attainment of a *Special Insight Meditation (Vipassana),* which severs the threads of delusions and realises both the wisdom of selflessness of person and the meaning of emptiness.

There are some traditions named after the *Ultimate View,* but before putting them into practice, one must begin with the first step. There is no *Great Perfection* without fulfilling the *Path of Accumulation.* One cannot experience true *Vipassana* or realise *Mahamudra* or *Dzogchen* without first accomplishing the Nine Stages of Calm Abiding Meditation. The former are the result of the latter. Talking about the *Ultimate View* without practising the fundamental precepts of the Buddha Dharma is putting the "cart before the horse".

This clearly reiterates the great Indian master Kamalashila's assertion of gradual attainment of enlightenment, which is not attained *suddenly.* As Sakya Pandita warned, there still appears to be some followers of Hwashang, the Chinese monk who challenged Kamalashila with his absurd notion of a *sudden approach.* One wonders why there are still some *Suddeners* with us after all this time, despite the refutation of the sudden approach so long ago. Perhaps this is a degenerate sign of the increase in the numbers of wild trainee elephant herds who are not receiving any actual training, not even gradually, let alone suddenly.

In summary, this illustration has one practical message for meditators and non-meditators: - *Traverse the path gradually like a turtle, not suddenly like a rabbit*!

Having spent six months attempting to achieve Calm Abiding in strict solitary retreat, under the guidance of His Eminence Choegye Trichen Rinpoche, the shining example of a great Tibetan master, I can assure readers that those who are able to give themselves a daily dose of Calm Abiding Meditation will experience a total shift in their perception of reality and a long lasting sense of inner peace.

BALANCING COMPASSION AND WISDOM

*The most effective method of dealing with
life's challenges is meditation.*

Lama Choedak Rinpoche

One thing we all have in common, is a wish to be of benefit and assistance to others. We do not intend to harm, or create difficulties for others, let alone ourselves. Instinctively, we have a lot of goodwill and willingness to help others, which we can offer in order to meet their expectations of us. We assume that what we do is good for both others and for ourselves. If we truly understand the relationship of cause and effect, we will realise that wholesome actions lead to positive outcomes: this is the law of karma. If we know the cause of something and create that cause, we cannot be disappointed with the outcome.

People who meditate will have a good degree of emotional intelligence and security. Emotional security is merit and merit is a stock of happiness. There is a sense of maturity and a stock of qualities, including love and compassion that stabilise oneself.

People who have merit do not have much room for sadness or anger. There is no vacant space for random ill-conceived thoughts to enter and take over. One will not need to keep some too close and others too far away. One will not feel impinged by others who are needy. One's mind is filled with love and compassion and the humility and dignity that are associated with them. One will receive letters which have nothing in them to remind oneself of their emptiness.

There are passionate people giving so much of their time and effort to be of service and benefit of others although people can also give for a long time with brooding anger and resentment. Due to a lack of wisdom, their generosity and kindness has turned into a cause of depression and bitterness. Meditation helps to increase our attention in all things we do so we avoid harm and the increase the benefit arising from our simple everyday actions. From parents to world leaders, everyone cherishes the wellbeing of those they love and care for and they wish to do things in the best possible way.

Prayers for the Practice of Calm Abiding Meditation

The following traditional Buddhist prayers are recited before commencing a session. Bow down three times towards the shrine, and with your hands at your heart recite: -

Refuge and Enlightenment Thought

In the Buddha, Dharma and Sangha
I take refuge 'til enlightenment.
By virtue of giving and the like
I shall reach buddhahood to aid beings. *(x3)*

The Four Immeasurables

May all beings have happiness and the cause of happiness.
May they be free from suffering and the cause of suffering.
May they never part from the happiness that knows no suffering.
May they dwell in equanimity free from attachment and aversion
to those near and far. *(x3)*

Prayer Before Teachings

According to the intelligence
And predisposition of each being
We ask that you turn the Dharma Wheel
Of great, low and common vehicles

Recite this verse three times at the conclusion of your session.-

Dedication

By this merit may we overcome
The defilements and gain omniscience.
May I liberate all beings from the
Ocean of birth, old age sickness.

Hearing the Mahayana teachings
Whatever merit I have accrued,
May all beings become stainless vessels
To hold the Mahayana teachings.

Courageous Manjushri knew all things
And Samantabhadra did likewise.
Following all of their examples
I shall dedicate all these merits.

May the excellent Bodhicitta
Take birth where it has not yet done so.
Where it has been born may it increase
Freely without degeneration.

SHAKYAMUNI BUDDHA MANTRA

The chanting of Shakyamuni Buddha mantra is a traditional Buddhist devotional meditation which calms the mind, arouses faith and blesses one's mindstream with mindfulness.

When chanting the mantra, imagine Buddha appears in the space in front of oneself. His body is the nature of light, golden in colour and blazing with the splendour of the major and minor marks of a Fully Enlightened One. His right hand is in the earth touching gesture and in the palm of his left hand he holds a begging bowl. As a monk in very beautiful robes he is sitting in the cross-legged lotus posture.

From his forehead radiates white light, his throat radiates red light and his heart radiates blue light which strikes one's forehead, throat and heart respectively. As a result, one's mindstream is blessed to never again be a source of harm and is implanted with the seed of the enlightened qualities of the body, speech and mind of the Buddha.

Tadyatha Om
Muni Muni Maha Muni
Shakyamuni Ye Svaha

DEVELOPING THE MOTIVATION TO MEDITATE

The following extracts are mainly from Shantideva's *Bodhisattva's Way of Life*, Buddhist sutras and some my own writings

Those who wish to guard their practice
Should very attentively guard their minds.
For those who do not guard their minds
Will be unable to guard their practice.

Unruly beings are as unlimited as space.
They cannot possibly all be overcome.
But if I overcome thoughts of anger alone
This will be equivalent to vanquishing all enemies.

Where would I possibly find enough leather
With which to cover the surface of the earth?
But wearing leather just on the soles of my shoes
Is equivalent to covering the earth with it.

Likewise, it is impossible for me
To restrain the external course of things.
But should I restrain this mind of mine
What would be the need to restrain all else?

Just as I would be attentive and careful of a wound
When amidst a bustling and uncontrolled crowd,
So I should always guard the wound of my mind
When dwelling amongst harmful people.

O you who wish to guard your mind,
I beseech you with folded hands
Always exert yourselves to guard
Mindfulness and alertness.

Whatever has been learnt,
contemplated and meditated upon
By those whose minds lack alertness,
Just like water in a leaking vase,
Will not be retained in their memory.

When mindfulness is set with the purpose
Of guarding the doorway of the mind,
Then alertness will come about
And even that which had gone will return.

With my vigour grown strong,
My mind should be placed in meditation.
For if thoughts be distracted,
We lie in the fangs of passions.

Short-lived yourself,
How can you think
That others, quite as fleeting
Are worthy of your love?

Thousands of births will pass
Without a sight of the one you love.
When unable to see your beloved,
Discontent disturbs your meditation.

When you have seen him,
Your longing, insatiate as ever,
Returns as before.
Then you forfeit the truth of reality.

Your fallen condition shocks you no longer.
Burning with grief,
You yearn for re-union
With the one you cherish.

Worries like these consume a brief life
Over and over again, to no purpose.
You stray from the Dharma eternal
For the sake of a transient friend.

To share in the life of the foolish
Will lead to the states of woe.
You share not, and they will hate you
What good comes from contact with fools?

Good friends at one time
All of a sudden they dislike you.
You try to please them, quite in vain
The worldly are not easily contented!

Advice on their duties stirs anger.
Your own good deeds they impede.
When you ignore what they say they are angry
And head for the states of woe.

Of his betters he is envious.
With his equals there is strife.
To inferiors he is haughty,
Mad for praise and wroth at blame.
Is there ever any goodness
In these foolish, common men?

Self applause, belittling others
Or encouragement to sin,
Some such evil's sure to happen
When one fool another meets.
Two evils meet when fools consort together.

Alone I will live, in peace and with unblemished mind.
Far should one flee from fools.
When met, they should be won by kindness,
Not in hope of intimacy, but to preserve an even, holy mind.

Enough for Dharma' s work I will take from them,
Just as a bee takes honey from a flower.
Hidden and unknown,
Like the new moon I will live my life.

The fools are no one's friends,
So have the Buddhas taught us they cannot love,
Unless their interest in themselves impels them.

With efforts our work is done and effortlessly it perishes.
Even though it is so, still you are not devoid of
Attachment to your work.
Desire is the root of suffering, impairing meditation and penance.

Desire is like a drink of salty water
Which causes thirst to increase again.
Because of the torments of accumulating, guarding and losing it,
Wealth should be known as boundless misery.

There is no opportunity for liberation
From the world's suffering
For those who are distracted
By the attachment to wealth.
Trees do not show disdain
And they demand no toilsome wooing.

Fain would I now consort with them
As my companions.

Fain would I dwell in a deserted sanctuary,
Beneath a tree, or in a cave
With noble disregard for all
Never looking back on what I left behind.

Fain would I dwell in spacious regions
Owned by no-one.
And there, a homeless wanderer,
Follow my own mind.

A clay bowl as my only wealth,
A robe that does not tempt the robbers.
Dwelling exempt from fear
And careless of my body.

Alone a man is born
And quite alone he meets his death.
This private anguish no-one shares
And friends can only bar true welfare.

Those who travel in *Becoming*
Should regard each incarnation as no more
Than a passing station
On their journey through Samsara.

So will I ever tend
Delightful and untroubled solitude,
Bestowing bliss and stilling all distractions.
And from all other cares released.
The mind set on collecting virtues.
My own spirit to unify and discipline
Will I strive.

Some pleasures are impermanent,
Deceptive, trivial and ruinous.
Avoid them as if they were poisonous vipers.
Their loss leads to much grief
And their gain never brings lasting satisfaction.
A man is lost if he expects contentment from great possessions.
They are unreal, unstable, hollow and uncertain.

MEDITATION ON DEATH
AND IMPERMANENCE

The following verses are from various Buddhist sutras, especially most
from Udanavarga. Elsewhere, it says laziness is the first obstacle and its
antidote is joyous effort. Reading these verses can greatly clarify one's
mind and whip the lazy donkey to run faster and safer than a racing horse.

The three worlds are impermanent like autumn clouds.
Seeing birth and death is like watching a play.
Life is gone like a flash of lightning,
Or a mountain waterfall.

As a budding mushroom shoots upwards carrying soil on its head,
So, I from birth onwards, carry decay and death with me.
Therefore, from the time of my birth onwards,
I move on in the direction of death,
Without turning back even for a moment.

Just as the sun, once risen,
Goes forward towards its setting,
And does not turn back for even an instant
From the path that it traverses,

Or as a mountain stream rapidly flows downwards
On its way, without ever turning backwards,
Death is now nearer than ever before.

All collections end in dispersal.
Whatever rises must also fall.
All meetings end in parting.
The end of life is death.

From the moment we enter the womb,
The journey from life to death begins.
Once begun, there is no turning back.

Just as brooks are extinguished by the summer heat,
Just as fruit falls from the tree early in the morning,
The stalks rotted by early morning mists,
The dew drops dispersed by the rays of the sun,
So this feeble body of mine, will fall apart in its turn.

Those people whose minds always desire
Family, house, money and wealth,
Just as a flood rushes through a town,
Are soon swept away by death.

Wherever you go there is no place
Where death cannot find an entry.
Not earth, nor sky, nor ocean deep,
Nor far within the mountain side.

As all ripe fruit falls and rots,
So all who are born are destroyed by death,
As every pot a skilled potter moulds from clay
Is finally broken and destroyed.

So, too is every person's life.
"When I have done this, then I will do that
And after that is finished, then I will do this."
Old-age, sickness and death consume

Those who make such preparations.
Whether one sits or moves, this life is irreversible.
Like a mighty river's course relentless through day and night,
Or like a herder with a stick, goading his flock into the fold,
Age and sickness drive all humans to their place of death.

Just as every step of a condemned man
Brings him nearer to the gallows,
Where he is doomed to hang to death,
So too is every person's life.All health ends in sickness,

All youth in old-age, all life in death,
All constructions in destruction.
Wherever one may dwell in the world,
One is struck down by the inevitable death.

If the diamond-body, the Rupakaya of the Buddhas,
Adorned with the major and minor marks of Enlightenment
Is impermanent, then my own body,
Which is like a bubble, is certainly impermanent.

Life is fleeting, and passes quickly,
Like a dew drop on the tip of a blade of grass
Which soon dries up when the sun rises.
Or like the bubbles of rain on the surface of a lake, which soon burst,
Or like a cow heading to be slaughtered,
Each time she raises her foot, she steps closer to death.

At day break many people can be seen,
By evening some are gone from sight.
At evening many people can be seen,
Next morning someone else has already passed away.

Some die when they are in the womb,
Some on the ground when they are born.
Some die just as they learn to crawl,
And some just as they learn to walk.

Some die old, some die young,
Some in the very prime of life.
How can I feel secure and think,
"I am young so I have long to live?"

Even though they had everything in life,
Many hundred thousands of men and women
From all walks of life have recently gone
Beneath the power of death, the leveller.

Your children cannot protect you
Nor your parents, nor your friends.
When the time has come for you to die,
You have no refuge except the Holy Dharma.

Like the flame of a butter-lamp
Shaken by a strong wind,
There is no certainty that this life
Will continue for even a single moment more.

The Lord of Death is not to be trusted,
For he does not ask whether one has finished or not.
Whether healthy or sick, I should reflect on The
certainty of death and uncertainty of its timing.

Lying on a bed, afflicted with disease,
Dry-mouthed, pale faced,
Feet and hands trembling,
Lips drawn back, teeth gnashing.

Not able to rise, one's lips emit a whizzing sound.
The body smeared with urine and excrement,
Unable to swallow the last mouthful of food and drink.

One sleeps in one's bed for the last time.
Sinking into an ocean of pain and agony.
Though surrounded by relatives,
Just as one is born alone into this world,
Alone one has to leave it.
One goes to the next world without any help from friends.

"Alas, death will come to me, but when is unknown.
Other than the Holy Dharma, and practising the virtues,
There is nothing to help me at the time of my death".

Until now, I have been distracted by mundane activities.
I have been attached to the objectives of this life alone.
I have held the insubstantial to be substantial,
And have not made full use of this precious life.

Nevertheless, I shall practise the Holy Dharma
From the bottom of my heart.
From now onwards without attachment to worldly activities.
I must do so consistently, without being swayed
By laziness and attachment to sleep.

If I do not practise the path of the Enlightened Ones
While I have this excellent opportunity,
Will I not be ashamed to let this precious life go astray
Like one who returns empty-handed from a treasure island?

About the Author

Lama Choedak Rinpoche was born in the yak hair tent of a nomad family on the Tibetan plateau in 1954. His family fled the Chinese Red Army invasion of their homeland to eventually re-establish their lives as refugees in Pokhara, Nepal, where they have remained for the last fifty years. Rinpoche took ordination as a monk while still attending high school and became the first Tibetan refugee to attain a Nepalese secondary education certificate.

As a novice monk Lama Choedak was accepted by the great Tibetan master His Eminence Choegye Trichen (1920-2007), one of a handful of monks helping to establish His Eminence's new seat in exile, at the birthplace of the Buddha, in Lumbini, Nepal. Rinpoche proved to be a particularly bright student and was close to His Eminence, acting as his personal attendant for six years. He completed twelve years of rigorous monastic training under Choegye Trichen's guidance, including a traditional three-and-a-half year solitary meditation retreat, which was sponsored by His Holiness the Dalai Lama.

Lama Choedak encountered many foreigners coming to Lumbini on pilgrimage to the Buddha's birthplace. He showed a natural flare for the English language and would go on to interpret for some of the highest lamas of Tibetan Buddhism. He was encouraged by Lama Yeshe to help bring Buddhism to the West and was a resident monk at a Buddhist centre in New Zealand in the early eighties. After some time, Rinpoche disrobed, maintaining his commitment to teaching as a lay Buddhist lama.

In the late Eighties, Lama Choedak settled in Canberra with a wife and young family, taking up a postgraduate scholarship at the

Australian National University. Being a qualified Tibetan lama with extensive monastic and retreat training, Rinpoche soon caught the attention of the few Canberrans interested in Tibetan Buddhism. In 1989, Sakya Losal Choe Dzong (SLCD) - the Tibetan Buddhist Society of Canberra - was officially launched and blessed by His Holiness Sakya Trizin in Canberra. In 1996, His Eminence Chogye Trichen came to Australia and launched Rongton Buddhist College at Evatt, ACT.

Rinpoche continues to promote the practice of Calm Abiding Meditation, acknowledging its benefits as a popular secular mindfulness technique, as well as recognising the importance of its Buddhist origins. Since 1996, he has conducted several 8-week meditation courses each year and a 10-day annual residential retreat, which have become some of the most popular events on the Australian Buddhist calendar. In 2001, Rinpoche began training some of his students to facilitate the Calm Abiding Meditation classes throughout Australia and New Zealand, a practise that he continues each year.

Rinpoche has been conducting Buddhist philosophy classes for more than fifteen years on a vast range of subjects and has published several books on the subjects of Buddhist philosophy and Tibetan history. He promotes the Vajrayana Buddhist meditation practices of the Sakya Tradition of Tibetan Buddhism, including Ngondro, White Tara and Medicine Buddha. SLCD has hosted many visits from high lamas including His Holiness the Sakya Trizin, His Eminence Choegye Trichen and Her Eminence Jetsun Kushok-la, all who have bestowed empowerments and given teachings. Rinpoche leads regular study and practice retreats on these special meditations and has translated many of the prayers and rituals into English.

Lama Choedak has published *A Textbook of Tibetan Language* for those learning the language and teaches weekly classes on Tibetan language, as well as conducting an annual Intensive Tibetan Language course.

In 2007, Lama Choedak returned to Tibet for the first time with a group of Western pilgrims. In order to fulfil his late teacher's wish, he reconnected with Nalendra monastery, the seat of His Eminence

Chogye Trichen. From this and subsequent visits, a humanitarian initiative called the *Nalendra Project* was founded, which has so far raised $180,000. This fund supports the wellbeing and education of 260 monks and nuns and helps maintain the traditional practices in five monasteries and nunneries in Phenpo Valley, north of Lhasa.

His Eminence Choegye Trichen regarded Lama Choedak as his heart son. In 2001, in recognition of his great contribution to the propagation of Buddhadharma in the West, and in particular the promotion of the Tsarpa tradition of the Sakya Lineage, His Eminence bestowed on him the title *Tsarpa Lochen Lama Choedak Rinpoche* meaning *Great Translator of the Tsarpa Tradition*.

Lama Choedak Rinpoche is a popular guest speaker and a regular participant on discussion panels during the visits of His Holiness the Dalai Lama to Australia. Excerpts from his public talks around Australia have been compiled into his bestselling book, *Healing Relationships*. Other books by Lama Choedak Yuthok include *Original Virtue* and *Lamdre - Dawn of Enlightenment*.

Sakya Losal Choe Dzong – the Tibetan Buddhist Society of Canberra - has grown to become one of the most established Tibetan Buddhist centres in Australia with two residential retreat centres and over a dozen sister centres. Most weekends, Rinpoche conducts residential meditation retreats, workshops and public talks at the invitation of Buddhist centres throughout Australia and New Zealand, including the SIBA Retreat Centre in East Gippsland, Victoria.

Lama Choedak Rinpoche's profound explanation of meditation and its everyday relevance is renowned for its lucidity, authenticity and humour. His teachings are offered from the heart, and spiced with the richness of his experience, dedication and realisation.

MEDITATION CENTRES

The following is a list of Buddhist centres around Australia and New Zealand hosting residential retreats, workshops as well as public talks conducted by Lama Choedak Rinpoche and other teachers.

These centres offer regular courses and drop-in group practice sessions in Calm Abiding Meditation.

Australian Capital Territory

Rongton Buddhist College
25 Alderman St
Evatt ACT 2617
mail@sakya.com.au | www.sakya.com.au
02 6238 2088

Victoria

SIBA Retreat Centre, East Gippsland
2592 Gelantipy Road
W Tree (near Buchan Caves) VIC 3885
siba@sakya.com.au | www.sakya.com.au/siba
03 5155 0329

New South Wales

Virupa Retreat Centre, Carwoola
179 Douglas Close
Carwoola NSW 2620
mail@sakya.com.au | www.sakya.com.au
02 6238 2088

Sakya Dolma Choe Ling, Sydney
7 Alexandria Ave
Eastwood NSW 2122
info@dolmabuddhistcentre.org.au
02 9801 3209

Tsechen Samten Ling, Umina
5 Haynes Avenue
Umina NSW 2257
nelson38@optusnet.com.au
02 4344 7718

Marpa Buddhist Centre, Forster
8 Wharf Street
Forster NSW 2428
www.marpabuddhistcentre.com.au
pandjmorgan@ozemail.com.au
02 6555 7167

Nesar Choe Dzong, Port MacQuarie
3/17 Wiruna Road
Port Macquarie NSW 2444
deborah.oldfield50@gmail.com
0402 911 905

Manjushri Buddhist Centre, Milton, NSW
40 Wason St
Milton NSW 2538
mbcmilton@gmail.com
0411 085 971 a/h

Queensland

Ananda Buddhist Centre, Rockhampton
Central Queensland Meditation Society
Cnr Hinchliff & Munro St, North Rockhampton QLD 4701
www.meditationcq.org | mail@meditationcq.org
0409 631 124

Chogye Padma Choe Dzong, Hervey Bay
Padma Buddhist Centre
6 Holiday Parade
Scarness QLD 4655
www.padma.org.au | info@padma.org.au
0417 940 121

Rongton Buddhist Centre, Brisbane
28 Farm Street
Newmarket QLD 4051
www.rongtonbuddhistcentre.org
rongtonbrisbane@gmail.com
(07) 3352 4730

Tharlam Ling Buddhist Centre, Townsville
13 Gill St
Kirwan QLD 4817
meditationtownsvilletharlamling | pheang@bigpond.net.au
07 4773 4223

South Australia

Tsechen Thubten Choe Ling, Adelaide
info@tsechen.org.au
08 8443 8823

New Zealand

Phunstok Choe Ling, Hawkes Bay, Napier
10 Herschell St
Hawkes Bay, Napier 4140 NZ
www.phuntsokchoeling.co.nz
phunstokchoeling@gmail.com
08 3294 108

Printed in Great Britain
by Amazon